The ADHD Student and Homework Problems

PATRICIA MCGUIRE

Published by Patricia McGuire MD, 2024.

THE ADHD STUDENT AND HOMEWORK PROBLEMS

First edition. January 19, 2024.

ISBN: 979-8224348336

Written by PATRICIA MCGUIRE.

Table of Contents

I would like to thank all the professionals who came before me. You helped me find these children and adolescents.

I would also thank the children and adolescents who took the time to tell me about their struggles and their wishes for help.

Preface

Raise your hand if you loved getting homework and were disappointed you had nothing to do.

Well, I see a few hands, but not many.

Why is that?

Could you feel mentally worn out after a day at school?

Did you need to do something "not learning" after school?

Were you hoping to have some downtime to go outdoors, watch an after-school special, read a fun book, or just lay back and relax?

If this is your child's daily truth, ADHD could be the reason. But most children with ADHD don't have "just" ADHD. They are called ADHD +. It is the +, which makes homework even more complex than if your child only had ADHD.

According to the CDC, approximately 60% of children with ADHD have at least one other disorder. The Learning Disabilities Association of America notes that 30-50% of students with ADHD also have learning disorders.

These co-existing disorders are where the problems with homework come into play. This book looks at the many factors affecting the ADHD student in learning and doing homework. It is essential to understand why children work to avoid their homework. This book will discuss the following factors that cause ADHD students to struggle with homework:

- Executive function skills
- Cognitive/mental flexibility
- Working memory
- Dysgraphia (written language problems)
- Language and communication problems
- Reading problems and dyslexia
- Organization and time management problems

- Strategies to help the ADHD student survive each day

Chapter 1: Who Is the ADHD Child

Six-year-old Joey has been diagnosed with ADHD. While medicine helps him stay focused in class and retain what he is learning, he still has some issues. One night, as his mother was putting him to bed, he shared -

" My teacher keeps telling me to keep my hands to myself. She says I am always touching things and other students.."

With tearful eyes, he asked his mother,

"When will anyone teach me how to keep my hands to myself?"

3-8% of the child and adolescent population is diagnosed with ADHD based on different assessment measures. But these numbers frequently refer back to when the term ADHD was introduced in the early 1980s and even before when it was called the hyperkinetic reaction of childhood and minimal brain dysfunction.

Recent literature reviews interview parents to see how many of their children have symptoms using a standardized checklist like the Vanderbilt. They also look at teacher ratings of the same children and adolescents. The literature also records how many youths have been diagnosed with ADHD or started on medication. The number of youth who are positive by checklist is closer to 10-15%. Healthcare providers prescribe ADHD medication to only 10-30 % of students diagnosed with ADHD.

Mildly impaired students may not be labeled until their abilities are exceeded by the demands around them, in middle school or high school. Others are obvious and identified early in elementary school or even in preschool for the more severely impaired. Approximately 70% will continue to have significant ADHD symptoms in adulthood.

ADHD is one of six neurodevelopmental disorders. Neurodevelopmental means that the brain develops with certain risks of conditions that impair different aspects of learning, language, behavior, and social interactions.

One child in six will have one of the six neurodevelopmental disorders. The six neurodevelopmental disorders are:

- Intellectual Developmental Disorder
- Communication Disorders
- Autism Spectrum Disorder
- Attention Deficit Hyperactivity Disorder
- Learning Disorders
- Motor Disorders

If a child has one of these disorders, there is a higher chance that he will have more than one. For example, 51% of students with ADHD also have reading problems. This co-existence of disorders is why it is essential to fully evaluate your child if ADHD is suspected.

Many professionals suggest treating ADHD first and then monitoring for learning problems. For the 51% of students with ADHD + Learning Disorders, this lack of a complete evaluation means that they will continue to stress out over school work. It means that home and school expect medication to be the answer. Anything less than excellent results will be blamed on the student choosing to do poorly on work, choosing to be sloppy and disorganized, and choosing to be non-compliant.

Treating all the symptoms/behaviors as due to ADHD can lead to frustration, failure, and a higher risk of your child dropping out of school, getting anxiety or depression, or becoming involved with drugs and alcohol. It is important to look for co-existing disorders to fully help your child.

CRITERIA OF ADHD

There are currently three presentations of ADHD, based on the Diagnostic And Statistical Manual, Fifth Edition of Mental Disorders (DSM 5).

ADHD 1 - INATTENTIVE

- Easily distracted, missing details, and forgetting things
- Difficulty maintaining focus on one task
- Becomes bored easily unless doing something novel or interesting
- Trouble focusing attention on the organization and completion of tasks
- Trouble completing or turning in homework, often losing it or other materials needed to do work
- Doesn't appear to be listening when spoken to
- Daydreams and becomes easily confused
- Trouble processing information quickly and accurately
- Problems following directions

ADHD 2a - HYPERACTIVE

- Fidgets and squirms often
- Talks nonstop
- Has problems with motor regulation, so they dash around and touch everything and anything
- Struggles to sit when needed
- Constantly in motion
- Trouble doing tasks quietly

ADHD 2b - IMPULSIVE

- Get impatient easily
- Blurts out answers, struggles to not over-show emotions
- Has trouble waiting in lines or for his turn in games

- Often interrupts conversations and other activities

ADHD 3 - COMBINED

To be combined the child must have at least six characteristics from presentation 1 *and* six characteristics from presentation 2.

ADHD is genetic, with only a few exceptions, which are being:

- Born prematurely

- Affected by iron deficiency anemia as an infant or toddler

- Experienced traumatic brain injuries

- Exposed to toxins in the brain pre- or post-natally, such as

  ◦ lead

  ◦ prenatal exposure to alcohol

  ◦ maternal smoking during pregnancy.

In order to fully help the ADHD student, it is important to understand how the other conditions interfere with the student's ability to do school work and homework. The following chapters will look at these conditions and make suggestions to help the student.

Chapter 2: EXECUTIVE FUNCTION SKILLS

ADHD and other neurodevelopmental disorders share problems in thinking, planning, and motor output. These abilities are controlled by executive function skills (EF).

Executive function skills relate to the brain's ability to do the following:

- Notice changes happening around it
- Process or understand what the changes mean
- Organize the body movements and materials to make needed changes
- Adjust to changes
- Monitor itself (brain) during tasks

These skills are needed throughout the child's day, whether at work, in academics, or in social-emotional situations.

Children are not born with fully developed EF skills. They develop over the first two decades of life. Your child's relationships and the world he lives in strongly influence the development of his EF skills.

Children with ADHD have problems in the development of these skills. Parents and teachers must have a great deal of patience to support the child with learning and integrating the elements of executive function into their daily activities.

According to the National Center for Learning Disabilities (NCLD), eight categories need development for a functioning EF system:

- Impulse Control (Inhibition)
- Emotional Control
- Planning & Prioritizing

- Flexibility (Shifting)
- Working Memory
- Self-monitoring
- Task Initiation
- Organization of materials

The Center on the Developing Child at Harvard University clusters Executive Function into three control areas or dimensions.
Cognitive/Mental Flexibility - which consists of

- Task Initiation
- Flexibility
- Organize materials
- Self-monitor

Working Memory - which consists of

- Working Memory
- Plan & Prioritize
- Organize materials

Inhibitory Control - which consists of

- Impulse Control
- Emotional Control

In later chapters, there will be further discussion on how problems with different aspects of EF can be helped.

Next, let's look at the role of temperament in how the student learns, behaviors, and responds to the world around him.

Chapter 3: TEMPERAMENT'S ROLE IN ADHD PROFILE

Everyone has a temperament profile, present since birth. Temperament is made up of our behavioral and emotional responses based on what is happening in the world around us.

There are nine traits of temperament:

- Activity level
- Rhythmicity
- Approachability
- Adaptability
- Intensity of response
- Basic mood
- Persistence (also called attention)
- Distractibility
- Sensory threshold

Each trait can be found at a very low or very high level of response. Temperament profiles don't change a great deal throughout life, although strategies can be learned to keep individual traits under more control.

Four of these traits, when very high on the spectrum, influence ADHD. These traits are:

- Rhythmicity
- Adaptability
- Basic Mood
- Persistence

Rhythmicity refers to the ability of the child to stay aware of the patterns and movement of time around him. It also refers to the ability to plan and organize himself and his materials.

Adaptability refers to how easy or difficult it is for the child to handle change, differences in opinions, and anything unexpected. This child will frequently ask "why" as in

- Why me?
- Why now?
- Why this way?

The child needs a concrete answer rather than the generic "Because I said so."

Basic mood refers to the initial response to situations. The negative end of the mood spectrum will find the child asking a number of "what if..." questions.

Persistence looks at the ability to stay on a task until finished. It also looks at the ability to multitask, moving back and forth between tasks without significant stress. For ADHD children, this is where they stop doing a task either because it is boring, or they don't know an answer or step, so they simply move on to another task.

Looking at how temperament affects ADHD, it is important to look at both Inattention ADHD and Impulsive/Hyperactive ADHD, since the traits have different levels of importance depending on the type of ADHD the child has.

Looking at the chart, Primary Traits refer to traits that rate highest for the type of ADHD. Secondary Traits refer to traits that are still high but lower than the Primary Traits.

For Inattention ADHD, the child struggles more with organization, recognizing patterns in life such as spelling, or traveling around the neighborhood. This is from Rhythmicity. He also finds it difficult to stick with a task if it isn't interesting or exciting. He may try to make it more exciting (like singing or doing some other activity at the same time). He may stop the task altogether if he has reached a point where he doesn't know the answer without asking for help and then begins doing something that he enjoys more.

PRIMARY TRAITS	ADHD INATTENTION	ADHD IMPULSIVE/HYPERACTIVE
	PERSISTENCE	ADAPTABILITY
	RHYTHMICITY	PERSISTENCE
SECONDARY TRAITS		
	ADAPTABILITY	BASIC MOOD
	BASIC MOOD	RHYTHMICITY

For the inattention presentation of ADHD, the two primary temperament traits that appear to affect homework are Rhythmicity and Persistence. For the impulsive/hyperactive presentation, they are Adaptability and Persistence.

Looking at the links with EF, the Inattentive ADHD presentation affects Working Memory Control. The Impulsive/Hyperactive presentation affects Cognitive/Mental Flexibility.

Adaptability and Basic Mood affect the inhibitory control area. When these last two traits are elevated, many children are labeled with Oppositional Defiant and Anxiety behaviors.

Rhythmicity and Persistence are processing skills, meaning they affect the ability to handle information coming in and creating answers or actions going out.

Adaptability and Basic Mood are limbic skills, meaning that they are handling the fight or flight responses of every change in a situation that the child encounters. This occurs constantly for all of us since we have to make decisions, consciously or subconsciously, on whether or not to respond to stimuli around us, and if we respond, do we do it with fear or confidence?

Both Rhythmicity and Persistence categories can be divided into one of two main groups or a combination group in an individual. With Rhythmicity the two main groups are the Deer in The Headlight group and the Time Checker group. For Persistence, the two main groups consist of The Bored Easily group and the I Have No Idea group.

In Rhythmicity, the Deer group is totally oblivious to what is going on around them. They don't feel time moving, they don't notice what is in their environment and don't see in their minds what they need to do to start or complete tasks. They are basically lost in time and space.

The second group, the Time Checkers, have the same problems but are aware of them and want to get a handle on the issues. But they need external accommodations to be successful. They frequently ask others to check on time, check on what to do next, if they are doing something correctly, etc. They will quickly latch onto systems to help manage and keep track of time and materials so that their internal anxiousness can be kept at bay.

Both groups find it very difficult to establish visual screens in their heads to handle some of this (like doing mental math or creating a mental list) but the Time Checkers will work to develop an external handwritten or other reminder object/list to compensate.

In Persistence, the Bored group are totally certain that they can do the task at hand but can't muster up the internal motivation to do it. They need external motivators to help move things along. In children with ADHD, the reason has been found to lie in the gratification/ motivation part of the brain, which does not develop as fully as a typical child. Because of this the ability to develop intrinsic motivation (such as "do it because you are supposed to") doesn't occur, or at least not until much later in adolescence or adulthood.

Helping The Pure ADHD Student

If your child has "only" ADHD, help is relatively simple. Most importantly, you will need to be his coach, mentor, and tutor, so that he learns the Executive Function skills. These are imperative in being able to successfully handle homework. To start, fill out this checklist of the core characteristics of ADHD combined, rating each characteristic 0-3. Zero means no problems, 1, occasionally, 2 often, and 3 all the time.

You can download a copy of this checklist here; ADHD Checklist[1] https://www.dropbox.com/s/abvvoq2ckvtkn3n/Characteristics %20of%20ADHD%20spectrum.pdf?dl=0

---

1.   http://www.dropbox.com/s/abvvoq2ckvtkn3n/ Characteristics%20of%20ADHD%20spectrum.pdf?dl=0

ADHD CHECKLIST

CHARACTERISTIC	SCORE (0-3)
Easily distracted, missing details, and forgetting things	
Difficulty maintaining focus on one task	
Becomes bored easily, unless doing something novel or interesting	
Trouble focusing attention on the organization and completion of tasks	
Trouble completing or turning in homework, often losing it or other materials needed to do work	
Doesn't appear to be listening when spoken to	
Daydreams and becomes easily confused	
Trouble processing information quickly and accurately	
Problems following directions	

Fidgets and squirms often

Talks nonstop

Has problems with motor regulation so dashes around and touches everything and anything

Struggles to sit when needed

Constantly in motion

Trouble doing tasks quietly

Get impatient easily

Blurts out answers, struggles to not over-show emotions

Has trouble waiting in lines or for his turn in games

Often interrupts conversations and other activities

Now you will look at the ADHD characteristics listed as 3 in the ADHD Checklist, putting them in the first column of the ADHD, EF, Temperament checklist.

You can download a copy of this checklist here: ADHD, EF, TEMPERAMENT[2]

https://www.dropbox.com/s/lspkc1a23hw8f07/
ADHD%20Temperament%20and%20Executive%20Function.pdf?dl=0

Next you will match them up to the Executive Function Dimensions (refer back to Executive Function section) and temperament traits that go with the EF Dimension.

ADHD CHARACTERISTICS WITH SCORE OF 3	EXECUTIVE FUNCTION DIMENSION	TEMPERAMENT TRAITS

For example, the characteristic of "Becomes bored easily, unless doing something novel or interesting" would be a persistence temperament trait. That means that it affects both Working Memory and Cognitive/Mental Flexibility Dimensions, although as an Inattention

---

2. http://www.dropbox.com/s/lspkc1a23hw8f07/
ADHD%20Temperament%20and%20Executive%20Function.pdf?dl=0

ADHD characteristic, it would most directly affect the Working Memory Dimension. In that dimension, we are talking about:

- Primary Working Memory – the ability to see in the mind's eye and juggle several pieces of information at the same time in one's mind
- Plan and prioritize - decide what needs to be done, and in what order of immediacy, and

- Organize materials - determine what materials are needed, and organize them on the desk, or in the bag to go home.

To help your child with these struggles, the following strategies will help in homework organization and completion.

COGNITIVE/MENTAL FLEXIBILITY DIMENSION:
Initiate & Shift -

• Have a routine that doesn't shift for homework

• Make a list of homework subjects and when each is due.

• Have your child check off each assignment when finished.

• Go over the instructions, making them step-by-step if needed.

• Divide up long-term projects into chunks that have due dates before the final due date.

• Using the model of 10 minutes of homework per night per grade (e.g., 4th grader has 40 minutes of homework per night on average), divide assignments up into timed segments on a visual schedule. Change assignments after the allotted time.

• Put a 5-minute break between assignments to recharge.

• If more time is needed for an assignment, complete the shorter assignments first.

• If each assignment takes longer than the allotted time on a fairly frequent basis, discuss with the teacher ways to keep the time demands in line with typical grade expectations.

Organize Materials & Self-monitor -

• Color coding for each subject helps with visual recognition of materials needed.

• Write down on a piece of paper what material will be needed for each assignment before starting.

• Look for similar needs per subject, and group them together (e.g., pencils, erasers, etc.)

• Put the subject book, worksheets, and material-specific tools together in one spot. Keep multi-subject materials in their own spot.

• As noted above, use the list of assignments to help organize and prioritize what to do first, second, etc. as well as chunks of longer-term projects.

• Schedule a 5-minute break at least every twenty minutes (depending on the child's grade) since ADHD students burn out quickly and need recharge time.

• Before considering an assignment done, it needs to be rechecked. Wait till all the assignments are done, so your child has time to process the info in the background of his mind as he does the other assignments. This will also allow all the subjects to be addressed before getting frustrated if changes are needed on one or more assignments.

• Be there while your child is doing his homework so off-task behavior can be redirected quickly.

• Allow for movement, talking, humming, etc. if it helps your student stay engaged with the homework. Studies have shown that breaks and movement both help with learning and processing, especially for ADHD children.

• Have your child check himself for on-task behavior at intervals. If off task, ask if he feels he needs a short break to stretch, focus on something else (including a different assignment), or get some background music that may provide a sense of pattern or rhythm to his thinking.

WORKING MEMORY DIMENSION:
Working Memory -

• Help your child develop visualization skills by having him create a mind picture of what he has heard or read. For example, for a word problem in math, have him draw out what the problem is saying. As he gets better at that ask him to describe it without drawing.

• Have your child explain to you the steps needed for an assignment or a task. For example, for writing a sentence, have him go over developing an idea, seeing the words in the idea, and seeing the mechanics of spelling, punctuation, and capitalization.

• Break down information into smaller chunks that are easier to remember, rather than one large chunk.

• Number your directions so he knows how much is needed (e.g., "I need you to get these 3 items..."

• Connect information to emotions, such as considering what would have been like for him as a child during the first Thanksgiving.

• Play card games such as Go Fish or Crazy Eights to actively engage the working memory. It requires your child to keep track of the rules as well as which of the cards have been used and the ones that are still in play.

Organize Self and Materials -

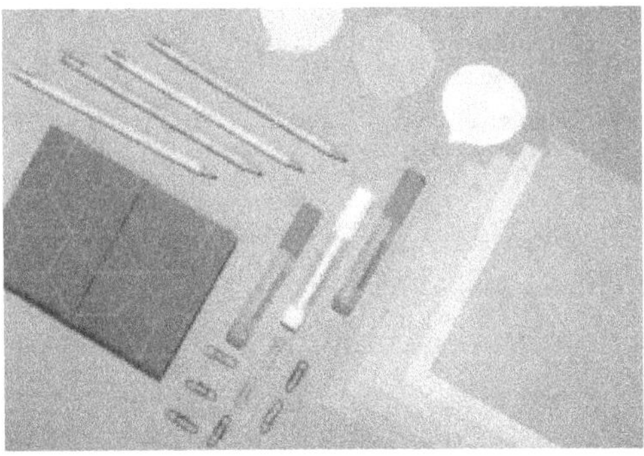

• Have an organized space for your student to do his homework

• From the assignment list developed above, number each as to the most important to do now (like a worksheet due the next day) and which ones can be divided over a few days

• Have your child estimate how long it will take to do one part of the homework. Write it down, start the timer, and then record how much gets done during that time.

• Don't stop if your child argues, just document that arguing took x minutes. Then note that even argue time is part of homework and determines how much time he will have for what he wants after he is done.

• Provide your student with reasonable motivators for which he will work. Children with ADHD have poor internal motivators and need external motivators to spice up the task

INHIBITORY CONTROL DIMENSION:

This EF dimension affects the quality of engagement your child has with his homework and other daily demands. When your student needs to keep his mind on his task or work, he feels stress due to the pull from the world around him in the form of distractions. He may also feel as if information is slipping out of his brain as you give instructions, or he is reading instructions on a worksheet. Because of this, he will frequently jump to a conclusion and begin working, only to find that he did it wrong since important steps were later on in the directions. This failure frequently leads to emotional outbursts.

Several parts of impulse control need your help for your student to improve the needed skills. Examples include:

• Teach listening skills - Use short, clear directions, giving one step at a time. Have him immediately repeat each step back to you. Ask him what the direction means and how he would do it. If he doesn't know, repeat it again, and change the pitch or volume of your voice to indicate important points, like action words (write, add, put away, etc.).

• Teach problem-solving skills - When your child gets stuck on his homework, he is likely to get frustrated and want to stop. Before that happens, sit down with him, and prepare him for that situation. Let him know that "when" he reaches that point in his homework, stop, come find you, and together you will brainstorm different ways to figure it out. Have him decide which option he wants to try first, staying with him in case there are sticking points, or coming back if needed.

• Model appropriate behavior for dealing with frustrations or other negative emotions – Show him that when you encounter a situation that could be upsetting you, pause, and verbally talk through what you are feeling and what your options are, including blowing up and possibly swearing. Then visibly take a deep breath, and verbalize why you are going to take a more controlled response to the situation

• Play impulse control games - Do you remember Red Light, Green Light? One person stands at the end of a room or yard with his back to a group of friends. He says "Green Light" and everyone tries to get to the end of the room/yard to tag you before you can turn around and say "Red Light". At the red light, everyone has to stop in their tracks like a statue, moving nothing until you turn away from them again and yell "Green Light." Another game could be Simon Says, where your child has to inhibit his action until he is sure that you said, "Simon Says.".

WHAT TO TAKE AWAY FROM THIS CHAPTER:

Your child with ADHD does not intend to make home life stressful. Homework, especially at the end of a long day of trying to keep up with school is like walking uphill against the wind. You now know some of the "whys" for this struggle. Important takeaways for interacting from this point forward are:

- You will need to provide a structure for him to develop his executive function skills.

- You should assume that the behaviors come from processing deficits, not oppositional behavior. This processing lag leads to anxiousness and rigidity. You must model calmness.

- Don't expect to tell your child something and that he will be able to remember and comply. Always provide visuals for follow-up.

- Number your directions whether given to your child verbally or visually to help with sequential deficits.

- Be there for homework to help him maintain organization and focus.

- Provide frequent breaks during homework so that his brain can recharge.

- Limit the total homework time to the established average of 10 minutes per grade per night (a slight increase can be provided if it is not a nightly occurrence).

In the following chapters, you will learn about other factors which can impact homework success. It is important to remember that only one child in three with ADHD is pure ADHD. The rest have additional conditions that add to homework stress.

Chapter 4: WRITING PROBLEMS DUE TO DYSGRAPHIA

DYSGRAPHIA EXPLAINED

Sally came home in tears from school again. When her mom asked her why, she replied, "My teacher made me stay in from recess to redo my work because she said she couldn't read it. But I had tried my best to get it all done before recess. When I focus on writing neatly, it takes too long. If I focus on writing quickly, my teacher can't read it. Why doesn't my teacher show me how to do both simultaneously?

Sally's teacher doesn't recognize that Sally has dysgraphia. Dysgraphia is a Latin word divided into two parts, dys- meaning difficulty, and graphia- meaning the writing process. This is part of Coordination disorder under the larger neurodevelopmental group of Motor Disorders. The problem revolves around less-than-optimal communication between the brain and the muscles used for fine motor skills. The rest of the Coordination Disorder includes larger muscles such as legs, feet, hands, and arms.

These are subtle fine motor skills difficulties, frequently missed in the early stages. Early problems can include difficulties picking up small items and tending to use more of a shoveling grasp rather than a pincer grasp. There can be an avoidance in drawing and coloring. Many children will find learning to tie their shoes difficult. Some also struggle with eating utensils.

Areas of Struggle with Dysgraphia:

Dysgraphia should be recognized as the student begins to learn how to write numbers and letters. He struggles to master the motor steps. His visual-spatial skills are lacking, affecting the legibility of his writing, such as with the size and slant of his letters.

Some students begin to write very small to compensate for the visual-spatial problems which make getting lines to the correct height, circles on the correct side of lines (b/d/p/q/g/9/6), and orientation (m/w/3) and (u/n) difficult. Frequently, the letters will have variable space with each other, sometimes overlapping, and other times having large spaces such as "t hi s". You may also note problems with writing on the lines and beginning at the left edge of the paper.

Many, if not most, students with dysgraphia can be identified by problems holding their pencil in a tripod grip (look at the picture at the beginning of this chapter).

The tripod grip has the index (2nd) finger on top so it can manipulate the pencil tip. The thumb and third fingers are on the sides, supporting and balancing the pencil for writing. The picture below will show one of the many ways that a student with dysgraphia may hold his pencil.

Looking at the written language skills, your child will likely have problems putting his ideas down on paper quickly and completely. He will have problems learning and applying capitalization, spelling, and punctuation rules.

He will also have problems proofreading his material for errors. As he monitors himself, he will likely erase his work frequently or try to write over misspelled words. Many children state and adults notice that it is much easier to say what they want to put on paper, than to actually get it on paper, somewhat like there was a blockage going from the brain down through the hand to the paper.

Impact of Dysgraphia on Your Child:

Dysgraphia makes putting schoolwork in a written format so challenging that it affects the student's academic performance. It is very hard to take notes, which requires multitasking skills of listening, visualizing the words, visualizing the mechanics, and engaging the hand to put it on the paper.

Dysgraphia can also affect your child's other life skills since the weak fine motor skills may affect tasks like zippering, tying shoes, buttoning, and using scissors. A number of children with dysgraphia also have a poor grasp of eating utensils, leading to messier eating.

Due to the problems noted for academic and life skills, many children with dysgraphia also have problems with self-esteem. Since dysgraphia is not understood by most teachers, your child is likely to hear that he is being lazy, sloppy, and careless. They become frustrated from having to rewrite work that they have already struggled to get on paper. Eventually, they avoid writing whenever possible, leading to poor grades from undone or minimally done homework.

How to Help Your Child with Dysgraphia:

You may find it difficult to have help provided to your child through school since dysgraphia is not always recognized. You can ask for an OT (Occupational Therapy) evaluation for fine motor skills and handwriting. This evaluation may allow your child to receive services to improve his handwriting. Many OTs use the Handwriting Without Tears program, which is multisensory in nature to enhance processing and memory. You may also ask for an evaluation of his written expression skills (mostly 3rd - 4th grade and above). Under an IEP, his resource teacher may use a curriculum such as Framing Your Thoughts (through Project Read), which is a multisensory way to master the mechanics and language of written expression.

If your child does not qualify under Special Education for an IEP (Individualized Educational Plan) but is still below either his peers or his own potential, based on his IQ, you could request a 504 Plan. This plan is a method, under the Americans with Disabilities Act (ADA), that calls for accommodations, modifications, and special services that will allow a student to function in a regular classroom.

It is different from an IEP in that an IEP focuses on direct instruction, while 504 focuses on other factors that affect academic performance.

DYSGRAPHIA & ADHD:

Since children with ADHD tend to struggle with the pacing of actions, even without dysgraphia, they frequently have messy handwriting. Many times their handwriting looks better when their medicine is in effect since it helps them take time to think about what they are doing with the pencil and also, they can hold on to their thoughts better. With dysgraphia, however, while there may be a little improvement in legibility, handwriting continues to be a problem, and written language takes a major hit.

You can help your student by breaking the writing task down into the following steps:

- Having the idea, or word he wants to write
- Visualizing the word or words he wants to write
- Visualizing the mechanics needed - spelling, capitalization, and punctuation
- Engaging his hand in the motor output to create the words or ideas on paper

Have him tell you the word, spelling it out loud if he can, which you can write on paper. This will then create a visualization for him. Now have him close his eyes and work to see the same idea or word that he had said out loud and you put on paper. Next, ask him to tell you where capitals and punctuation go for his idea. Finally, have him start writing it, but allow him to reference what you wrote down since he may have problems keeping it in his working memory when he is struggling to get it on paper.

As your child gets older and has to write more for assignments, such as reports and essays, use graphic organizers to help him remember (and store as a peripheral brain) before he begins to put together the piece. You can find ideas for graphic organizers by doing a Google search for Graphic Organizers. You will likely find images that you can then adapt to your child's needs. You can also find more resources by going to the LDA (Learning Disabilities of America) site, http://ldaamerica.org/graphic-organizers/.

For taking notes in class, which would be mostly middle school and above, you may want to consider purchasing the Livescribe Smartpen.

There are various options, but the basics are that the pen records the lecture as the student takes what notes he can. Later he can put his pen on the special paper it uses to the information he wants to remember and he can hear the lecture. From there, he can further add to his notes, aiding in recalling and consolidating information in his brain.

You may find that your child struggles with both handwriting and keyboarding due to his dysgraphia. In this case, you may want to look into Speech to Print software. The one historically used the most often is Dragon Naturally Speaking. But an article published in November 2023, https://zapier.com/blog/best-text-dictation-software/ looked at the (writer's opinion) best dictation software for 2024 listed these programs:

- Apple Dictation[1] for free dictation software on Apple devices
- Windows 11 Speech Recognition[2] for free dictation software on Windows
- Dragon by Nuance[3] for a customizable dictation app
- Google Docs voice typing[4] for dictating in Google Docs
- Gboard[5] for a free mobile dictation app
- Otter[6] for collaboration

Dragon (not free) is still listed, but the Apple and Windows free software led the list. There is a learning curve for all of the software choices, but they are quick learners. Definitely worth looking into for longer writing assignments.

---

1. https://zapier.com/blog/best-text-dictation-software/#appledictation

2. https://zapier.com/blog/best-text-dictation-software/#windowsspeech

3. https://zapier.com/blog/best-text-dictation-software/#dragon

4. https://zapier.com/blog/best-text-dictation-software/#googledocs

5. https://zapier.com/blog/best-text-dictation-software/#gboard

6. https://zapier.com/blog/best-text-dictation-software/#otter

Accommodations and Modifications for a 504 Plan:

• For your child it may be the use of a computer or tablet so he can type rather than write with his hand, although even typing is more of a challenge than for a typical student, but less than handwriting.

• Some children need to go a step further and use speech to print software to dictate what they want to put on paper.

• Your child may be able to better put his ideas on paper by printing rather than cursive, which would be a modification.

• Modified assignments, requiring less writing, but maybe have him use pictures, dioramas, or oral presentations can be offered.

• For homework, you may write down the answers your child gives you to decrease his frustration. You could also type it on the computer, print it, and staple it to his worksheets.

• Your child would benefit from activities to lessen muscle fatigue in his hands. This would include shaking his hands before and during writing or rubbing them briskly together, to decrease cramping.

• Have him strengthen his hand muscles by playing with clay and doing activities requiring small muscles, like picking up rice kernels, holding rows of pennies in the palm of the hand, and even sewing.

WHAT TO TAKE AWAY FROM THIS CHAPTER:

Children with ADHD are frequently labeled as being lazy, uncooperative, and unmotivated. This is unfortunate since what may be happening is that their other learning and motor struggles are being misinterpreted. With dysgraphia, one has to start out assuming that the child wants to do well but needs further direct help. Your role is to help and advocate as needed for these accommodations and, if necessary, evaluations to clarify his writing struggles.

Chapter 5: LANGUAGE AND COMMUNICATION PROBLEMS

Charlie was not happy. He had lost recess again because his teacher thought he was being disrespectful. She had given the class directions for an assignment. He thought he understood and did it as best he could. After he handed it in, she came to his desk and with an irritated voice said, "Charlie, I am tired of your horsing around on assignments. You were supposed to write about <u>which</u> character in the story was the antagonist. There was <u>no witch</u> in the story. You can just miss recess for this."

What is one area in which your ADHD child gets into trouble a lot? Could it be talking to others? Sounding rude, sassy, or boisterous?

Children with ADHD tend to have many problems with language. In an article published in 2014, 40% of children with ADHD had language problems. Less than 1/2 of these children had received speech-language services and only 1 in 4 were currently receiving services. This study didn't look at the types of language problems these children had, using only a screener to find the children with both problems. A more formal evaluation would be needed to figure out if they had vocabulary (receptive and expressive), problems with grammar or semantics, or problems with pragmatics.

Problems with pragmatics come under the label of Social Communication Disorder. If your child has this diagnosis you will notice struggles with knowing the right time and the right person to share information with. They frequently don't notice or respond to social cues, such as facial expressions, body language, or even tone of voice.

The studies reported in the last 5-7 years have frequently used a tool called the CELF-4. This looks at both receptive and expressive language skills. These studies were from clinic-based populations, meaning that they had searched for help rather than identified by their schools. One study identified ADHD students as having language impairments if they scored 2 or more Standard Deviations (SD) below the mean, the level most often used for providing services in school districts.

Many students, however, are between 1 and 2 SD below the mean, indicating that they are still struggling but not to a level where government funds are provided for services. Schools frequently mislabel these "fall-through-the-crack" students as behaviorally disordered. Scores at this level will definitely affect academics and social interactions.

Sources of Language-based Problems:

Characteristics of language-based problems lie in auditory processing and impulsivity. The auditory processing deficits affect both receptive and expressive language.

Below are frequent areas of problem with auditory processing:

- Struggles with short-term auditory memory
- Problems following directions
- Slow processing speed when dealing with oral and written language
- Problems focusing on listening when in a busy or noisy environment
- Problems with reading comprehension

Impulsivity affects language processing and use in the following ways:

- Planning on what to say
- Organizing one's thoughts
- Putting information and thoughts in a coherent sequence
- Be able to recall what had been learned previously

Language-based Behaviors - Receptive:

So, what are the behaviors associated with receptive language deficits? How many does your child show?

- Difficulties remembering numbers, words, or lengthy materials

- Struggles to interpret ambiguous information, containing idioms or in a joke format

- Problems during class lessons getting the correct information - getting details but not the main idea, leading to tangential or off-task responses or questions.

Language-based Behaviors - Expressive:
What are the behaviors associated with expressive language deficits? How many does your child show?

- Whether speaking or writing tends to invert syllables or words

- Struggles with retrieving words in conversation

- Problems expressing emotions effectively

- Struggling with rambling conversations

- Problems expressing his thoughts effectively, in both speaking and writing

LANGUAGE & ADHD:
Communicating with others requires time to organize thoughts, connect with the level of emotion needed for the moment, and control of the message's speed and volume. It also requires a strong understanding of how word choice lets the other person know what you mean.

For children and teens with ADHD, these are hard to do both because of impulsively blurting out and the frequent problems with vocabulary and language skills.

To help your child, it will take patience to listen past the words to understand the intent of what was said. The wrong choice of words can lead you to think that he is being rude. Problems with longer communication such as going back over information, and correcting what was first said, may lead to the belief that your child is not being honest, or may be trying to cover up something which could get him into trouble. Unfortunately, the truth is that he frequently retrieves information from his memory in a disorganized manner.

As he hears himself tell you the facts, he recognizes the errors and attempts to correct himself. Responding to him with irritation or anger leads to his brain getting stuck in the limbic system (fight or flight panic) creating more errors in recall and retelling. It becomes a vicious circle.

In my practice, I have found that by putting what I understand on my whiteboard as pictures, I can be sure I understand, and if need be, change the picture to clearly show what he is trying to tell us.

Above is an example of how I use the whiteboard to help understand and provide language options to children with ADHD and other challenges. This image shows a typical situation dealing with others on the playground. I will go through it with the child, first asking him what he did and how it turned out.

I will then ask him if anyone has ever suggested another approach and go through with him how that might turn out. I always write the options we talk about on the side so we can refer back to them as often as we need. I continue to ask him about other strategies that he or others have thought about and how they may play out. When he gets to the "I don't know any other ways" I then say that some other children I work with have suggested <u>X strategy</u> and ask him if he has ever heard of or tried it. Most likely he hasn't so we go through that strategy and possible outcomes on the board too.

Having a visual to provide a common understanding of meaning and sequences allows your child to feel safe and willing to try other options.

The whiteboard or other visual aid bypasses your child's difficulty in trying to see the situation in his head and replay it exactly the same way each time a strategy is explored. This method is also very useful for finding out why something went wrong, how to do a task, and why to do it in a certain order. You are providing your child with a visual and language means of understanding and being compliant with needs, directions, and expectations.

You can use the whiteboard to deconstruct words or language, thus increasing understanding Here are some suggestions:

- Have your child draw a picture of what he wants to say in a sentence. It helps organize his thoughts, much like a graphic organizer, which by the way can be used with the visual.
- Have him tell you as much as he can about a word: color, size, shape, sound, purpose. This improves his ability to express himself
- Have him draw each of those elements of the word to reinforce the meaning.
- Have him change one element and see if that changes what the

word means (does color change what it is or just what type of "what" it is).

- Bring out the Thesaurus to try other words in sentences to see if the meaning stays or changes somewhat.
- Find online games to play that will improve your child's vocabulary or language skills. One example found by Googling "language games" is http://www.funbrain.com/words.html.

Source of Language Problems & How to Help:

Between 6-35% of children with ADHD (depending on the study) have a history of early language delays. This is significantly more than in non-ADHD children where the rate is between 2 to 5.5%.

Russell Barkley Ph.D., an expert on ADHD, also theorized that there was less self-directed speech, internalization of language (saying out loud without realizing it), and problems with higher-order executive functioning needed for goal-directed behavioral guidance and planning.

So, what can you do to help your ADHD child? There are several activities found at Linguisystems (http://linguisystems.com) that may help. The following are examples of products from Linguisystems that could help you expand your child's language skills:

- Figurative Language Card Games (ages 10 to adult)

- HELP series (ages 6 to adult)

- 10 Quick Play Folder Games (ages 4-13)

Online resources include:

- https://www.speechandlanguagekids.com

- http://www.enhancemyvocabulary.com/

- http://www.vocabulary.com/

What you will find from these resources are tools to help you teach your child the language skills he needs to succeed. It will require that you model, practice, provide positive feedback on progress, and combine vocal and visual methods of sharing information.

WHAT TO TAKE AWAY FROM THIS CHAPTER:

In summary, there is a good chance that your child with ADHD will have some difficulties with language. When helping him with homework, provide time to model language for thinking through assignments, ask questions to increase concentration on the material, and provide visual reinforcement for your child to use as often as needed.

Chapter 6: READING PROBLEMS AND DYSLEXIA

Annie didn't like school. She was in a special reading class because she couldn't figure out the words on the page. Her teacher told her to work harder, but she felt like she was working as hard as she could and yet nothing changed.

She could never get the sounds and letters to go together after she had sounded out words. She liked it so much more when her mother read to her so she could understand how to do her homework.

While having ADHD is enough of a struggle for children in school for academic success, what makes it worse is that up to 50% also qualify as having a reading disability (RD). Now this is a level where the school provides reading interventions through Special Education. Many more could also have problems at a lesser level.

When you look at RD, most have dyslexia, a neurologic, language-based disorder of phonemic and phonologic awareness. Studies do show that 30% of students with dyslexia also have ADHD (on the flip side 14% of children with ADHD have dyslexia). The rest of the reading struggles are due to either other language-based problems or cognitive processing problems due to working memory issues and troubles with sustained attention. When you notice your child with ADHD showing problems with reading, it is essential to request an evaluation earlier rather than later due to the high numbers noted above.

You may not be able to receive a school evaluation if they don't feel it is severe enough, so you should find out who is available in your area who evaluates for learning problems. Check with your state's branch of the International Dyslexia Association, http://www.eida.org, or Learning Disabilities Association, http://ldaamerica.org/[1] for any such providers

---

1.   http://ldaamerica.org/

in your state. Understanding where your child is struggling with reading will allow for a more focused intervention.

What Areas May be Deficient for Your Child

- Phonemic awareness - understanding of the role of sounds in spoken and written language.

- Phonologic awareness -understanding of the rules of sound order in connection with letter and letter groups. It affects, for example, understanding words, divisions of syllables, and rimes.

- Working memory - being able to keep sounds or words together while handling further incoming information. This issue with working memory can lead to problems remembering what was just read or how to combine the sounds of the word that your child just decoded.

- Problems keeping on the correct line when reading

- Low receptive vocabulary skills which affect comprehension of the passage

- Low receptive language skills which also affect deeper levels of understanding of a passage.

How Can You Help Your Child with Reading

If your child has dyslexia, you will notice many problems with awareness of sounds in words. You may notice this with listening, speaking, and spelling. They may be to different degrees. A few children have more problems recognizing or visualizing the correct letter(s) with the sound they hear or see.

The first subtype of dyslexia noted above is dysphonetic, while the second subtype is dyseidetic (which is sometimes called surface or visual dyslexia). That means problems with sounds or images/letters, respectively. It would require someone with more in-depth knowledge of dyslexia to identify the dyseidectic child because he may function in the low average range for phonetic skills.

Children with dyslexia need explicit teaching to become aware of the sounds in words and language, how to manipulate those sounds, and how to correctly connect the sounds with the alphabetic symbol(s) that go with the sound. One way to help is to find a person trained in multisensory structured language (MSL) approaches to reading. They may have their training in programs such as one of the following:

- Orton Gillingham
- Slingerland
- Project Read
- Wilson

- Sonday

There are other programs too, found by downloading the Matrix of MSL programs from the International Dyslexia Association (http://www.eida.org/additional-resources/[2]). All of them focus on using multiple senses simultaneously to teach reading and spelling.

These are –

- <u>listening</u> to hear the sounds,
- <u>saying</u> to feel the sounds,
- <u>looking</u> to recognize the letters that go with the letters that go with the sounds,
- <u>and writing</u> to feel the letters that go with the sounds.

Providing activities with words to improve the fluency of these skills will help your child. You can purchase resources to help, such as from Linguisystems (http://www.linguisystems.com)[3].

Look for products that are geared to phonemic and phonologic awareness.

The types of skills that these activities will focus on are:

- <u>Rhyming</u> - recognizing and generating

- <u>Segmenting words</u> - using clapping as your child says each syllable in a word

- <u>Syllable & Sound Blending</u> - put sounds and syllables together to create a word

- <u>Initial & Final Alliterations</u> - Be able to identify the first and last sounds in words

---

2.   http://www.eida.org

3.   http://www.linguisystems.com

- <u>Phoneme Isolation</u> - Present a one-syllable word to your child and then say a sound in the word. Your child has to say if it is the first, last, or middle sound

- <u>Sound and Syllable Deletion</u> - Have your child say a word and then for multisyllabic words ask them to say the word again with one of the syllables missing. For a single-syllable word, have them say it again with one of the sounds missing.

- <u>Phoneme-Grapheme Correspondence</u> - Show your child a letter or letter group and have the child produce the sound that goes with it.

The next problem area is working memory, which negatively impacts reading comprehension. This problem is because there is a need to simultaneously remember and understand, which requires sustained attention and effort during the task.

There are many important skills to teach your child, but first you must make sure your child is willing to read. To do that, select materials of high interest to him, so that working on decoding and comprehension will seem less like a punishment.

Once you find reading materials that your child likes, help them by developing these skills. You can then encourage him to use these same skills with less interesting, but assigned reading:

- <u>Minimize Distractions</u> - Reducing distractions may require a quiet location or using 'white noise' to control the auditory environment.

- <u>Chunk the Reading</u> - Have your child only read for a few minutes at a time, then take a break to move around and refocus. Taking a pause will allow the information to finish processing in your child's mind instead of just backing up and waiting for the previous information to get through.

- <u>Use a Bookmark</u> - A bookmark will help your child keep track of where he is reading and use it to track each line so he doesn't skip lines.
- <u>Active Reading Strategies</u> - Have your child use active strategies such as underlining and note taking. These strategies may be for slightly older students (3rd grade and above).

• <u>Color to Enhance Recall</u> - The contrast of color with the traditional black print on white paper will attract the eye and attention of your student. Use colored pencils with the colors coded by you as to what they are highlighting (e.g., Vocabulary yellow, actions red, etc.) and colored post-it notes to write down important facts.

• <u>Get a Spare Book</u> - In order to take notes or highlight you may need to purchase an extra book of his own. Alternatively, if there is an eBook version, buying that will allow the student to bookmark, highlight, and, as needed, listen to the material.

• <u>Preview Content</u> - Look ahead so you can go over key concepts, topic, characters, vocabulary, and preview the subheadings of each section before he begins to read.

• <u>Subvocalize as Reading</u> - Encourage your child to quietly read out loud since being a more active way of learning, improves comprehension

• <u>Monitoring Understanding</u> - Teach your student to check frequently on understanding by paraphrasing what he has read, in his own words, so you know he understands. It will also reinforce comprehension.

• <u>Creating Images</u> - Have your child create a picture in his head of what he is reading to increase understanding and comprehension. Using visual aids like story maps, and diagrams can increase understanding.

The last areas that can cause difficulties with reading comprehension are receptive vocabulary and language skills. Receptive means understanding what is coming in. For receptive vocabulary, it is understanding the meaning of words as labels, actions, or emotions. For receptive language we are talking about understanding the combination of words that have varied levels of meanings depending on the grammar and semantics (analogies, idioms, metaphors, etc. and context.) It also means understanding that multiple words, such as sad and unhappy, could describe the same thing. Many children with ADHD are more concrete and literal in understanding labels, leading to confusion with figurative language and words with more than one meaning, such as seal, which can mean close securely, or the name of a sea animal.

Helping your child depends on his age. Kindergarteners up to 2nd graders enjoy games such as I Spy, using either one of the books, or wherever you might be (grocery store, mall, etc.) Reading books to your child will expose him to words that are not in his day-to-day conversations. Spend time discussing the vocabulary and sentence meanings, page by page, and what the story was about as a whole.

READING & ADHD:

A key problem with ADHD deals with the ability to focus and maintain that focus to accomplish a task. This means learning to read and using reading to learn are both at risk for creating academic under performance. Starting in the early elementary years, until your student has mastered the foundational skills you should start homework with the following:

Warm up for reading by going through the phonologic elements, such as sounds for /a/, /sh/, /str/, and /oa/ for example. You can get the complete list of these elements by buying the Language Tool Kit and Cards (https://shop.epslearning.com/ and look it up in search - you want the one that says & Cards). With these cards, you have him hear what you say, then he says it, then show it to him, and finally, have him write the letters that go with the sounds. After he can recognize how to say the sound without you saying it first, move up to just saying and writing what you show him on the card.

You can mix it up by sometimes playing a phonics game before starting the homework. There are some free games at www.education.com/games/phonics. Playing educational games before work will engage your ADHD child since it is more exciting and motivating.

After the warm-up, begin the homework with reading, since he has the information at a more conscious level of his brain, making it more easily accessible. Depending on how you prioritize the homework, have him use these skills as often as possible.

If your child does not have problems with decoding/pronouncing/spelling words, the focus should be on comprehension. Frequently students with ADHD rush through directions and passages, not focusing on the meaning of the words and phrases that they are reading. You will need to help your student slow down to read for meaning, so he doesn't end up having to reread (which is "boring") to get the meaning.

Initially, you will have to discuss with him what the material will cover before he starts reading the information. For instructions, it will be about telling him what he needs to do. As he reads the instructions, have him pause and underline the action words (verbs or predicates) such as "underline all the words that begin with /th/".

For reading assignments, discuss what the topic is about before starting. Have him guess what the author may do next. If it is social studies, have him guess what the people in the country or state may do for a living, etc. As he reads, have him stop and repeat what the sentence is about (the subject), underlining the action words again and either you or he put them on a separate sheet of paper. Have him put a line on the page and then fill it with the object (what receives the action). You can discuss with him any adjectives (words that make the subject and object more specific to this sentence, such as "the large dog", and "the hot flames") and how they help you tell the difference between similar words in different stories.

WHAT TO TAKE AWAY FROM THIS CHAPTER:

Learning to read and take meaning from it is hard for children with ADHD. These struggles with co-occurring dyslexia, language problems, or comprehension problems are due to the need for sustained attention and focus on decoding and meaning.

By taking the lead in making sure your child masters the skills that focus on sound awareness in words and language, reading with intention of understanding, and keeping visually on target will provide your child with the tools to successfully move through school. You are a member of your child's team. Be there to help him become a reading star.

Chapter 7: ORGANIZATION AND TIME MANAGEMENT PROBLEMS

Since only one child in three with ADHD has no other problems, you need to anticipate having to modify whatever you are doing to help them with homework to meet multiple needs. That is why I spent time going over the other problems that can occur with ADHD. Now you will focus on how to work on these issues while helping your child develop good homework skills.

ORGANIZATION & ADHD:

As was mentioned earlier in this book, organization is very important. Organization includes the space your child does homework on, how he uses his folders, and the order in which he does his homework.

Because most individuals (not just kids) with ADHD do not have a good feel for time and space, you will need to bring those to his conscious level every time you are doing homework with him. I recommend thinking of time in several levels:

- Minutes - roughly how long should your student be expected to do homework every night? A formula quoted for years is 10 minutes of homework per night, per grade. So, kindergartners have 5 minutes, 1st grade 10 minutes, 2nd graders 20 minutes, etc. This time refers to actually working on homework. It is not an activity you can do with your child to reinforce his learning, such as games and activities.

-
    - Hours - how many hours from when your student leaves school until bedtime. Your child will likely complain that you are always taking away his free/play

time. Unknowingly you may be doing that by the other activities that fill a typical school week. But there is a way to make sure that there is some time for down-time for your child because this is extremely important for ADHD children in order to recharge.

- To help keep track of this time, either as a vertical list, or as a round clock, put down each obligation from coming home to going to bed. Set a time limit and location for each obligation, such as 4:30 to (x min/grade)for homework, 5 to 5:25 for supper, etc. If there needs to be changes during the week, make sure you show it to your child on the visual, explaining that it will not be there every night, but may be there one night a week such as soccer practice, gymnastics, etc. Then consider trimming a little bit of time off of other obligations, so he still gets a little down/play time.

- Days - This fits in with the hours but shows how each day may have minor differences from each other, although there is an overall organization or schedule. Review this daily. It would help if you put any long-term projects or activities, such as book reports, music programs, etc., on these days.

- Weeks - Help your child sense the sequential nature of time and the repetition of sequences, which is what weeks do. This way, he will learn that there are patterns, such as swim class always being on Wednesday, tutoring always being on Tuesday, etc. The more your child can begin to notice and predict patterns of time, the less lost in time he will be.

- Months - This is a longer time concept but allows for learning how there can be patterns of occurrence over longer time periods. He can begin to see that he goes to the dentist 2 times a year, once every 6 months. He will begin to anticipate the months that give him the most free time - Summer.

- It will also help him see the repetitive sequence of time over a larger canvas of life.

- Years - This is where the big events occur infrequently, such as birthdays, Halloween, and Christmas (or Hanukkah or Kwanzaa.)

After going through the time aspects, work with your student to figure out what tools he needs to have to complete his homework. Have him say what he can remember, writing it down as a list. Ask him what he would need for any part of his night's assignment if he doesn't list it at first. If he doesn't know, ask a little bit more specifically to see if it will trigger a recall in his memory. If not, ask if item X would be needed and add it to the list.

Have him put in front of himself, only what is needed for the particular assignment he will be working on at that time. When it is done, ask him to see what will be needed for the next assignment, putting away anything that is not needed. Repeat for each part of his nightly homework. This, over time, will create a ritual that will keep him organized.

When his work is done, have him put it in the appropriate folder, labeled as "Give to Teacher". Many parents make the mistake (I know I did) of labeling it "Take to School". It got to school but then came right home again, because it was not clear what to do when the work got to school. ADHD children can be very concrete and literal so we have to help them by being clear.

As your child does his homework, have him do it in small chunks. Using chunking will give him time to process what he is doing rather than just rushing through to get it done. It will also not drain his brain as fast since there will be a gap where recharging can occur. Taking a break for a few minutes after doing that chunk will lead to improved storage and consolidation, especially if there is a little review when starting again to work on the next chunk.

WHAT TO TAKE AWAY FROM THIS CHAPTER:

It can be tiring and overwhelming working with your ADHD child on homework. He requires much more one-on-one attention to achieve foundational skills for studying, learning, and skill building.

I have had more than one parent say to me "I didn't think parenting would be this hard." It is hard, but the successful, confident adult that occurs at the end of the journey is worth it. You can do it, just take it a chunk at a time.

Chapter 8: STRATEGIES TO HELP THE ADHD STUDENT

Jack found that he could get more done if he was allowed to wiggle. But his teachers and parents didn't believe this, continually telling him to "Sit still and pay attention." He would try to focus on sitting still but then his work would suffer. If he focused on getting his work done, he got into trouble for wiggling. He was so frustrated.

When working with your ADHD child on homework, you need to consider strategies that are not academic but help address your child's needs. These need to be considered as part of his daily life events in order to help him have as much control over his ADHD as he can.

EXERCISE:

There have been multiple studies over the last several years, including one in the Journal of Child and Adolescent Psychiatry in 2015, which showed that creating more opportunities for physical activity improves attention and behavior. Countrywide there has been the use of activity balls on a base in classrooms to replace chairs. These allow for more controlled movement while working. These can also be useful for when your child is doing homework. It is not the only option, however. The Parent Science article Exercise for Children: How Physical Fitness

Benefits the Brain — and Helps Kids Learn[1] (https://parentingscience.com/exercise-for-children/) describes various options to increase physical and mental activity to keep a mind energetic and engaged.

Another option for your child while he is doing homework is to set a clock for 10 minutes. When it goes off, your child gets up, begins bouncing on his feet and takes 20 very slow, deep breaths in and out. This lowers stress, increases energy, and increases the amount of oxygen going to his brain as he thinks. After he is done, the clock is sent again to repeat the process.

NUTRITION:

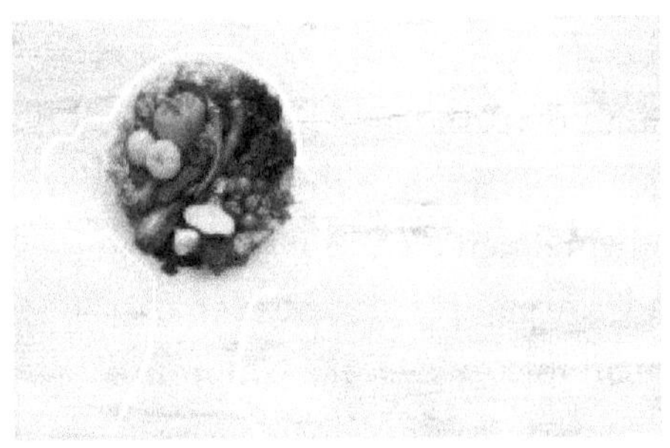

The nutritional value of a child's daily meals is vital since poor nutrition leads to many problems. For your child with ADHD, it becomes much more important to understand what helps and what makes his behaviors and focusing skills decline. Highly processed foods, most with high salt and fructose corn syrup, tend to be stored as fat. They also create a boomerang effect in blood glucose, the brain's primary energy source. This rollercoaster blood glucose leads to irritability, focusing problems, and restless behavior. So, what can you do to maximize your child's nutrition for home and school success?

Protein:

The average protein intake for children should be 24-30 grams per day. For adults it is 45-70 grams. Several studies over the last couple

---

1.   https://parentingscience.com/exercise-for-children/

of decades have shown that ADHD students who have high protein breakfasts and lunches function better in the classroom, both behaviorally and academically (due to more sustained focus). Ideally, it should not be part of a highly processed product. Since an 8-ounce glass of milk (regular or soy) contains 7 grams of protein, it is not that hard to do. You could also give your child one ounce of cheese (like one mozzarella stick) or an ounce of meat (such as 1/2 serving of a cold cut such as chicken or 2 servings (2 slices) of bologna - but this has more preservatives).

Omega-3 Fatty Acids:

While there are still questions about the value of omega-3 fatty acids in improving ADHD symptoms, there has been enough evidence to suggest that it is worth trying.

One study found that students did better with the EPA part of the omega 3 fatty acids, more so than the DHA part, which unfortunately is the part that is being marketed more for helping ADHD. This study found that around 750 mg per day of EPA over a period of 3 months showed improvement in core ADHD symptoms.

Besides supplements, you can increase your child's Omega-3 fatty acid intake by using flaxseed (2 tablespoons)which provides 133% of daily recommended intake (DRI). Flaxseed can be sprinkled on cereal (hot or cold), added to baking, or be part of a smoothie.

Walnuts also supply more than 100% of DRI, with just 1/4 cup of walnut pieces, again making it part of different dishes or by themselves.

Minerals & Vitamins:

More and more studies are showing that insufficient levels of certain minerals and vitamins affect health, brain functioning and thus ADHD. The following list of minerals currently need to be optimal to help students with ADHD, whether supplied as supplements or through food:

Zinc - insufficient levels lead to problems with impulsivity and hyperactivity. Getting blood levels to where they should be will help these two areas, although it does not affect inattentiveness. You should, however, ask your physician to get a blood zinc level before starting, since high zinc levels can be dangerous.

Foods that contain higher levels of zinc include:

- Beef - 4 ounces has 37% of DRI
- Lamb - 4 ounces has 35% of DRI
- Sesame seeds - 1/4 cup has 25% of DRI
- For more options check out nih.gov/factsheets/Zinc-HealthProfessional/[2]

<u>Iron</u> - low iron levels have a negative effect on all brain functions including learning and attention. Children who don't eat many iron rich foods, are at high risk for this. Again, check with your physician to check serum ferritin levels, which may be low even if your child is not actually considered anemic.

Foods that contain higher level of iron include:

- Spinach - one cup has 36% of DRI

- Beef - 3 ounces has 11% of DRI

- Cereals - check the box, but iron-fortified cereals may have up to 18 mg which is 100% of DRI

- For more options check out nih.gov/factsheets/Iron-HealthProfessional/[3]

<u>Magnesium</u> - This mineral is helpful with stress and anxiety. For ADHD students, it also increases relaxation and sleep.

---

2. https://ods.od.nih.gov/factsheets/Zinc-HealthProfessional/

3. https://ods.od.nih.gov/factsheets/Iron-HealthProfessional/

Since sleep is a major problem for children with ADHD, making sure that he gets sufficient magnesium can be important. If you are considering supplements for this, have your doctor check blood levels first.

To do it through diet, look to increase his intake of green, leafy vegetables, nuts, and legumes. If your child doesn't care for green leafy vegetables, they can be mixed with fruits into smoothies. Pineapple and apple juices can be used to sweeten the taste and cover some of the green taste. You can hide navy and black beans in stews, tacos, or tortillas.

<u>Vitamin C</u> - In addition to helping with immunity, Vitamin C helps with dopamine, one of the essential neurotransmitters affected by ADHD. Ideally to help your child, using foods that contain Vitamin C can be beneficial, although supplements help too.

It may be hard to believe, but it is found not just in oranges and pineapples. The largest amount of Vitamin C is in papayas, followed by bell peppers, broccoli, and Brussels sprouts. Other fruits with good Vitamin C levels are strawberries, kiwi fruits, and cantaloupes. One thing to remember, whether taking Vitamin C in food or by supplement, is that Vitamin C can inhibit the absorption of ADHD medications, so take it during a one-hour window before or after taking the ADHD medication.

Screen Time:

On average, children are exposed to screen time 7 hours per day. As far back as 2004, studies have shown that screen time (in this case TV) between ages 1 to 3, resulted in 10% having significant attentional problems by age 7. Newer studies continue to show that too much screen time, which now includes all the possibilities such as Nintendo, X Box, and online, creates an increased need for constant enticement to maintain engagement. There is no time to process deeper levels of options and possible outcomes or consequences. They also lead to increased adrenaline with the action games that stimulate the limbic system of the brain into a prolonged fight or flight response. This response shows up as the increased irritability shown by your child when asked to stop and even after stopping a video game.

Technology can benefit learning and review, but again, reinforce limits so there are times for person-to-person interaction. Even with a shift to educational media, too much time at the expense of interpersonal interaction can create problems. The current AAP (2016 American Academy of Pediatrics) recommendation is for no more than 2 hours per day of screen time. However, this AAP 2-hour/day screentime recommendation was made before the explosion of iPads, tablets, and smartphones use at home and school.

Since 2016, the AAP has continued to recommend monitoring children's screen time, but with the use of computers in school and for homework, a strict time limit is more challenging to define.

An important issue to address is the need to keep screens out of the child's bedroom. This refers to TVs, tablets or computers, smartphones, etc. It is too tempting to go to these distractors rather than sleeping. Lack of sleep leads to more problems with attention, learning, and behavior. So no matter why your child has had these devices in his bedroom, they need to be removed to allow your child to succeed.

SKILLS TRAINING:

Mindfulness:

How do you get your child to focus on one thing at a time? First teach him to focus on his breathing. Okay it is a little more complicated than that, but it is the first step into the practice of mindfulness, a form of meditation. I have been doing a variation of this for almost 20 years to help ADHD and other students gain more control over their emotions. You may have noticed that any time your child is experiencing any emotion other than calm, there is some sense of anxiousness.

You will likely see some fidgety movement, or your child may begin to slouch, put his arms closer to his body, maybe even crossing his arms across his chest. You may hear him beginning to complain, argue, or say he can't do whatever it is that you want him to do. These are anxiety-based behaviors. He may fear failure, loss of time to do what he finds preferable to what he is supposed to be doing, or that it is a punishment or unfair parenting compared to a sibling. These all are anxiety triggers.

One activity that you can do with your child is to get a toy that has glitter in it such as a snow globe or if you can find one, a glitter tube where you can watch the glitter slowly sink to the bottom of the tube. Before shaking the globe or tube, have your child notice something on the other side - not inside - to focus on.

Then have him shake the globe so that the glitter is really swirling. Tell him to watch until he can see the object that he focused on beyond the globe again. Let him know that the swirling glitter is like his brain when he is not focusing on the one important thing. As he slows himself down to notice his breathing the swirling in his head will begin to slow. He can focus on the essential tasks when all the ideas, thoughts, worries, etc., have settled in his brain.

Another activity is to use rhythm as found in music to demonstrate how to think and then pause to process. To do this, clap three times and have your child then clap three times. Next clap 2 times, due a rest equal to one clap and then do a 3rd clap. Have him repeat that. Tell him that the silence (rest), called a pause, is what he needs to do periodically during the day to provide his brain with a chance to quiet or calm down. To show him what happens if he doesn't, have him clap continuously for 2 minutes. Ask him how his hands feel. Are they tired? Do they sting a bit? That is what his brain feels like without the pauses to rest.

WHAT TO TAKE AWAY FROM THIS CHAPTER:

Working on homework with your child with ADHD requires understanding the many aspects of your child, both of the ADHD and of the other conditions which lead to more difficulty in getting started and completing homework. In this chapter we looked beyond the books and worksheets to the body and mind. If your child isn't optimal in his whole-body wellness, he will find it more challenging to engage in work and continue when tired.

WHAT TO TAKE AWAY FROM THIS BOOK:

Despite what you may hear from those who don't have an ADHD child, or who feel that your child has to just "get over it", you <u>ARE</u> needed to provide support, guidance, and advocacy for many more years than a child without ADHD or another of the neurodevelopmental disorders (remember Chapter 1). But this support, given without resentment, will allow your child to grow into adulthood with better self-esteem and more belief that work does lead to the outcomes he wants.

The End.

Don't miss out!

Visit the website below and you can sign up to receive emails whenever PATRICIA MCGUIRE publishes a new book. There's no charge and no obligation.

https://books2read.com/r/B-A-CSUCB-LLVTC

BOOKS 2 READ

Connecting independent readers to independent writers.

About the Author

Dr. Patricia McGuire is a developmental and behavioral pediatrician. This means that she can explain how kids develop and learn, and "why" they do things the way they do. She helps parents understand their child by building a profile based on a combination of his temperament, any learning or developmental struggles he may have, and the effects of his community on his functioning.

You may enjoy her book, Never Assume: Getting To Know Children Before Labeling Them

Keep up with Dr. McGuire through social media:

FACEBOOK: https://www.facebook.com/profile.php?id=100076017596913

Read more at https://helpingchallengingchildren.online.